SONGS FROM MY HEART

SONGS FROM MY HEART

poems and photographs by

Daisaku Ikeda

translated by

Burton Watson

WEATHERHILL
New York & Tokyo

This book, in both its original Japanese version and English transla-
tion, was first published, in deluxe editions, in 1976 by Seikyo Press,
Tokyo, on the occasion of the publisher's twenty-fifth anniversary.

First English trade edition, 1978

Published by John Weatherhill, Inc., of New York and Tokyo, with
editorial offices at 7–6–13 Roppongi, Minato-ku, Tokyo 106, Japan.
Copyright © 1976, 1978 by Daisaku Ikeda; all rights reserved.
Printed and first published in Japan.

Library of Congress Cataloging in Publication Data: Ikeda, Daisaku. /
Songs from my heart. / Translation of Waga kokoro no uta. /
I. Title. / PL853.K33W2913 1978 / 895.6'1'5 / 78-3560 / ISBN
0–8348–0133–7

Contents

For some years now it has been my custom to record in the form of poems various ideas and emotions that come to me, giving them as free expression as possible. Goethe once remarked: "All my poems are occasional poems, suggested by real life, and having therein a firm foundation." My own poems too may be said to spring from real life, or more specifically, from the daily whirlwind of activities that I, like any ordinary person, find myself engaged in.

Embodying feelings that have come to me in the course of my association with friends or my talks with young people, these poems have been jotted down over the years in my diary or in odd corners of my notes. Most were composed while I was traveling about in the cause of peace, or in moments of leisure before retiring at night.

For this reason, I suppose there are some that, in form at least, hardly seem like poems at all. And yet they are all frank expressions of basic human emotions, and I wonder if that is not the true definition of poetry, regardless of the form it happens to take.

I confess I have considerable qualms when I think that these poems of mine in English translation will come before the eyes of readers in numerous countries around the world. But if they are read merely as messages from a plain individual who strives at all times to be an honest human being, then I will be gratified.

As for the photographs, these too are mine and were taken in much the same spirit as that in which the poems were written.

In closing I would like to express my thanks to Burton Watson, adjunct professor of Columbia University, for the pains he has taken in making the translations, and to the editorial staff of John Weatherhill, Inc., for their labors and patience in producing the book.

Tokyo, Spring, 1978   D AISAKU I KEDA

Translator's Note

Since I am not a specialist in Japanese poetry, I do not feel competent to comment on the literary significance of these poems. But I would like to say a word about how the translations were prepared.

The editors of the original volume selected the poems and supplied me with texts, from which I made the first tentative translations. I then met with them and discussed the translation of technical terms and other key words. Mr. Ikeda often writes in classical Japanese, which is quite different from the modern written and spoken language, and he also employs a highly poetic and elliptical style. Consequently, there are passages in his works that are capable of varying interpretations. In my translations, I have attempted to convey as faithfully as possible the interpretation that was explained to me.

I could probably have made things somewhat easier for the English reader if I had been freer in my rendering—if I had, that is, paraphrased the meaning of the Japanese rather than sticking to the exact wording of the original. But it seems to me that poetry, unlike prose, depends not so much upon the ideas themselves as upon the precise words and images used to embody them. I have therefore tried in most cases to be as literal as possible.

The originals contain almost no punctuation, and I have consequently kept punctuation of the English to the bare minimum needed to prevent misunderstanding. In a few cases notes have been added at the end of a poem to assist the English reader in understanding allusions and unfamiliar terms; these are based on information supplied me by the original editors.

9

SONG OF YOUTH

Though clouds dot the sky
and the wind blows
the sun rises again today
The eight a.m. sun of youth
holding within itself limitless power
as it spreads its light abroad, advances on correct course

Never deviating from its strict orbit,
beyond mansions of the sky, filling the heavens,
a king in glory
the sun advances wordless, unspeaking

Wisdom that is in fact ignorance, decline of culture
mechanization of man, death of philosophy
scheming authority, deceit, trickery—
is it not to dispel these
that it sends forth its golden rays
that it advances in this lordly manner?

A sculpture of men and women in their entanglements
a globe whose contentions never cease
a world caught in the agony of indecision and revolt
human existence, the brilliance of its life all but extinguished
beneath the machinery of oppression—
the sun advances through the heavens
drawing forth a new vitality

The Buddhism of Nichiren is like the sun
our faith too shall be the sun
To give true proof of regeneration

filled with inner anger we advance
upon the great road of reason, sincerity, and wisdom

At last we have come to recognize it—
the challenge to become a true human being
It is the fight for the human revolution
that begins with one individual
and swells now to a multitude of seven million

In that region, in this region,
in that office, in this family
friends fight, friends win
The delight in these open faces, rolling forth in countless
    waves,
has become a third force

Friends who walk proudly in a life of self-affirming joy
friends of unlimited creativity, singing of the culture of the
    common people
friends who fight bravely to transcend the theory of class
friends who struggle tirelessly and without end to give shape
    to the new life
friends who tread an unshakable path, in a glory rooted in
    society
friends who are victorious in the family revolution, who
    jingle the bells of good fortune

Steadfastly we advance
in the sincere and bloodless battle of the century
The forces of emotionalism, panic, and envy
have become three cowardly enemies
blocking the path of our lordly peace
Their jealousy

churns like sand, rages like a storm
But we will never be afraid
We bear the banners of eternal life
and we shall advance once more
We lift high the banners of revolution

Oh
the Buddhism of Nichiren is the philosophy of youth
Facing the strongholds of reaction and hatred
mounted on white horses
dauntlessly the columns will go forward

The curtain has opened on the second decade
Moving no longer in a line but over a broad surface
you work to build the towering and fruitful
culture of the twenty-first century
This will be the stage upon which you perform!
This will be your debut!

I have my mission which is mine alone
You too
have a mission which only you can fulfill

Without the strength of youthful activity
what can the older generation accomplish?
Upon the slope of construction, from incompletion to
    completion
with songs of youth
melodies of culture
sounding the gongs of innovation
heroically, rain-battered, let us work on

With bright eyes
soft smiles
brawny muscles
red-cheeked, clean-browed
tenacious in individuality
clad in the work clothes of steadfast determination
you commence the construction of the total revolution

The steel is cold and there are lashing winds
The steel is heavy—your sweat pours out

But only out of this labor and mission
will the true value of human life be born
and the music of a magnificent fruition ring forth

We young people will fight
Striding through the storms of meanness, flattery, and carping
along the road of true belief
so that a myriad flowers may bloom,
out of the valleys of darkness
so that we may reach the high peaks of justice,
from the rigid society of our times with its sighs
to create a splendid era of human flowering
like that of *Man'yōshū* times
we will move forward, we will work!

The formula for the enrichment of human nature—
it exists nowhere but in
a complete and all-embracing faith
The profound search for a meaningful life—
it exists
in a faith that is lofty

The self-won victory over anguish—
it is none other than
the religion of the Lion King
A life unshakable in the face of strong winds—
it can be attained
only through a faith that is pure

There are difficult paths of error
mazes of mistaken belief
young people who subscribe to no theories
arrogant scholars—
But the inevitable, the finest achievement
lies in a proven religion alone

Facing the eastern sky for the morning prayer
pressing palms together solemnly
to the source of the myriad beings,
an awesome epitome of the universe in miniature

With this act as the point of origin for growth and development
in the midst of the varied forms of reality
in the midst of mankind's variety and complexness
like the eagle, king of creatures that soar the sky
like the lion, king of creatures that walk the earth
we advance, mounted on the winged horses of freedom
In our right hands gripping the profound principles of the
    holy wisdom
in our left embracing the compassion of the Lotus, racing,
strengthening the ranks of our solidarity,
through freedom of choice and conviction, once more we
    advance

What is our goal?
It is *kōsen-rufu*
In pursuing it we must surmount countless obstacles
This dedication and the long campaign to spread the teachings
shall be our lifelong journey

For us, there is no stopping—
we are like the flow of a mighty river
There may be those who,
beguiled by pleasant dreams, turn back along the way
There may be those who,
shunning the steep path to the peak,
blithely return to the lights of the bright city

We, though,
will go forward gallantly in the face of the storm
In order to build the city of Eternal Truth
bravely we will work to clear the great dense forest
Valiant youthful seekers of the Way
we put aside womanish feelings, manfully push ahead
Without undue optimism, without sentiment
we advance ever toward the ultimate point of our destination

Now, along the true path, bringing Buddhism to society
flanking our column
many are the friends who soar aloft

In the anger-filled world of politics
in the culture of the heavenly beings
in the scholarly world of the *shōmon*

there are many paths, branching many ways,
yet all come together at the rugged mountain of *kōsen-rufu*

Despite skirmishes and retreats
the main body of troops never falters but advances in order

Laying down the foundation for the total revolution
our main force advances earnestly, imposingly

At times quietly observing
the movements of society
at times working in harmony with society
deeply, broadly advancing
at times advancing in fury
through the river of slander and abuse
at times, putting on the armor of endurance,
we advance to the duet of silence and dialogue
And at other times
to defend our doctrine
we risk death in a fight of pure and utter resistance
The progress of good health
wild dance of peace
in time to the march of the revolution of new life
we move

My friends!
we have been brothers from the infinite past
My friends!
we, each in our lives, are brothers and sisters
The latent bonds of comradeship that bind us
no man
no stratagems of any kind
can ever sunder

Now the curtain has fallen on one act of the century
Factionalism and clashing interest

egoists and trickery
shadow figures and irresponsibility
injustice and domineering authority
foul politics, visible and invisible—
can young people in their purity go along with these?

Only the beauty
of naturally formed solidarity
which transcends these,
the wheels that roll forward toward the happiness of mankind,
from these splendid wheels
these wheels that revolve with life's vitality,
from them shall come the society of the true human republic

Solidarity of the common people to preserve the dignity of
    life
solidarity of blood and tears that fights off every form of
    oppression
solidarity of hearts built out of idealism and good faith
true wheels of mankind—
though we face the criticisms of prejudice and ignorance
we stand tall in our pride

These worthy groups built
by men themselves, for the sake of men,
through the power of fundamental law and the ultimate truth

Never playing up to authority,
never compromising with the powers of wealth,
blueprints for a great popular current
brilliant with philosophy, science, and culture—
this will be the final chapter of our human building

To liberate society from confrontations,
responding to all cultural demands,
a renaissance of the twenty-first century—
this we proclaim as
our great cultural movement

In the past there have been different kinds of revolution
political, economic, educational
But when one type of revolution is carried out in isolation
it lacks solidity, gives rise to strain and onesidedness
A political revolution alone
calls forth bloodshed, insures no safety for the populace
and once again those in authority lord it over the masses

Likewise economic revolution
fails to fulfill the hopes of the people,
the penniless commoners are trampled underfoot in a process
    of meaningless change
A revolution in education only
again is no blessing to the people—
it cannot bear up before the turmoil of the world's shifts
    and movements

What the people long for
to carry them through the twenty-first century
is no reorganization of external forms alone
They desire a sound revolution
carried out within themselves
gradually and in an atmosphere of peace
founded upon the philosophy and beliefs of each individual
This calls for farsighted judgments
and a profound system of principles

This is what I would name a total revolution
and it is this
we call *kōsen-rufu*

If there are those who would laugh
let them laugh
if there are those who would disparage
let them disparage

For us at the end of the broad road we travel
the history of countless centuries of the future waits to
   give its proof
A monument to mankind's far-off glory and victory
waits for us

Dear comrades!
my beloved young people!
in this belief together we will advance with joy!

In the land of freedom
in America too
hundreds of thousands of friends are at work
In the countries of the future
on the African continent too
thousands of friends are coming to join us
In our brother lands
of Southeast Asia too
we have many friends waiting
To India too, land of neutrality
to South America, to the country of the Incas
to Australia, the island continent
the True Buddhism of the world has spread
In the countries of Europe with their age-old culture

we have friends who fight
In the Soviet Union, republic of the people
and finally in our neighboring land of China
friends will soon appear

Passively, actively
the world awaits us

With the ideologies
of all races, all countries
as a gateway and means of understanding,
the religious movement of renovation shall go forward

The support of complete knowledge
the foundation of complete democracy
the soil of a complete culture—
to complete the task of bringing these about,
Young people!
wave the banners of the world religion of freedom and peace

Never forget that these banners
must wave only upon foundations
that day after day are firm and unyielding

To accomplish this, young people,
I ask you today again to carry on friendly dialogues in the
    very midst of the people
My young people!
take time from your busy schedules,
listen carefully to the voice of your friend in trouble

because to be clear and full of confidence
like the blue sky and the sun

is what qualifies you to be glorious young revolutionaries
There are other banners, renowned but false in name—
in time their colors will fade
There are medals adorning the societies of false goodness
but their glow is lifeless, not a bright human light
There are politicians, false figures
who sooner or later will be unmasked by the perceptive
    young

There are those who see only the reality of the present
and those who see the eternal in the present reality
We choose to be the latter, and from that standpoint
manifest ourselves, shining in glory

Fame, medals we have no use for
Simple human beings, in the palace of our flesh
we walk the pleasure-filled road of life
Along the golden road that will never crumble for eternity
as unfamed, uncrowned human beings we walk on

Once more, young people, my friends!

With the present century as our stairway
let us go forward toward that mountain of the twenty-
    first century
stoutly, vigorously pulling our way up
we will open again the curtain
upon a new century's development

Young people!
you must go on living
Above all, you must go on living

As chief figures in the brilliant total revolution
resolutely you will achieve your victory in history

The eight a.m. sun of youth
today again is rising!
It is rising in time to the beat of youth!

Notes: Man'yōshū *times (p. 16) indicates the period in early Japanese history reflected in the* Man'yōshū *(The Collection of Myriad Leaves), the earliest anthology of Japanese poetry, compiled in the eighth century. The poet is thinking in particular of the Nara period (710–84), an era of great cultural and artistic achievement.*

The lion (p. 17), king of the beasts, is often employed in Buddhism to symbolize persons or writings of the highest eminence.

Kōsen-rufu *(p. 18) means to secure lasting global peace by propagating true Buddhism and bringing people to enjoy indestructible happiness.*

The shōmon *(p. 18) or* sravaka, *is one who attains enlightenment by listening to the Buddha's teachings. He represents the seventh of the ten stages of existence and is characterized as a scholar. Though some Mahayana sutras deny that the* shōmon *and* engaku, *or* pratyeka-buddha *(the eighth of the ten states), can attain true buddhahood, the Lotus Sutra insists that they can.*

LOOKING AT NATURE

MORIGASAKI BEACH

With my friend by the shore
Morigasaki
pungent seaside smell
waves withdrawing

nineteen-year-old boys
pondering what path to choose
philosophical talk
as the hours go by

My friend troubled
always so poor
"The way of Christ
is the one I'll follow!"
eyes flashing keen in the moonlight—
to that firm heartbeat
the waves roll in

On the crumbling embankment
grasses grown thick
voices of insects—what kind I don't know
Tonight shall we fashion
poems and songs?
music with a tone
of ancient court times?

But my friend stands silent
What way should I choose,
that my life may wing away
to far-off gardens of the moon?
He wipes away the tears, sighing

My friend in lonely sorrow
I too
but with one boundless aspiration:
Make a promise with me
we'll face life
whatever pain it brings!
My friend smiles
"I'll go along with that!"

That far-off world
my friend is seeking—
a different one
but I too have my Way
A long song on a stage
that never ends
till hair turns white,
talking with the moon

I wish you all luck
my friend!
Next time we meet—
when will it be?
Wordless we depart
upon our separate journeys
silver waves sway gently
Morigasaki

Note: This poem was written in August, 1947, when the poet was nineteen. Morigasaki Beach, on Tokyo Bay near the poet's home in Ota Ward, Tokyo, was at that time a quiet, pine-grown shore area where he often went walking. The friend in the poem worked at the same ironworks as did the poet.

SPRING BREEZES

The sudden shower has passed,
the spring breezes rustle

Blossoms of the cherry-apple
wake from sleep,
one petal dancing

By the rocks in the garden
the shimmering
heat waves rise

On the surface of the pond
a leaf boat
glides quietly along

I pray that
the spring breezes of good fortune
blow in the hearts of all

ATSUTA VILLAGE: THINKING OF
MY MASTER'S CHILDHOOD HOME

Atsuta Village by the cold northern sea
amid endless snowstorms
that silver house by the seaside, poor as it was,
that was your ancient castle of glory

Atsuta River with the poetry of spring and summer,
herring-filled waves of the Japan Sea,
this region opened up by the lords of Matsumae,
sheer cliffs, fishing-village gardens

The boy unmoving, beneath the bright full moon,
reading works of biography and history,
on the ruddy cheek sadly a tear
music of a heart that beats with uprightness

Atsushi cloth sewn by a white-haired mother,
with her painful needle saying "Overcome injustice!"
In response to her prayers the young phoenix
soars to heaven in search of a rainbow

The father too, chatting by the stove,
mending his nets, the wrinkles of his smiling face—
"A brave man marches forward to face the winds of authority"
this is the motto, the song of father and son

"Old home in Atsuta—I will not forget you!"
Bearing northern winds with him, the youth
from a nameless land embarks on his long journey,
setting forth for the sake of the world

*Notes: Atsuta Village in Hokkaidō was the childhood home of Jōsei Toda,
the second president of Sōka Gakkai and the poet's teacher.*

*Atsushi cloth is made from tree fiber and was originally produced by the
Ainu people in northern Japan.*

32

BLOSSOMS THAT SCATTER

Cherries in bloom that the air raid spared
blue sky above them   fallen petals jumbled

for a background the gutted ruins of reality
and the pitiful people who cannot look up to them

bitter are their long wanderings
the road of parent and child

amid the waves of little shacks, flowers in bloom
cherry blossoms—is theirs the hue of dawn?

Ah, there is a simile in this existence
men of power and men of peace

"blossoms that scatter, blossoms that remain
to become blossoms that scatter"—so sings a man

blossoms of youth, how many million—
why must they scatter? why must they scatter?

In distant southern seas, ill-fated cherries
full bloom not yet on them, their branches are in pain

and my friends remaining, their hearts, before we know it,
wounded by the loss of the world of the ideal

Are all things impermanent? are they eternal?
without even knowing, must we scatter?

◀ *Cherry blossoms, Nara*

Blossoms that scatter, blossoms that remain,
bloom forever, in spring send out your fragrance on the
storm!

Note: In April, 1943, when the poet was seventeen, Tokyo's Ota Ward, where the poet was working in an ironworks, was heavily damaged in an air raid. The poem was composed when the poet observed the cherries blooming among the charred ruins of a temple in the area.

THE SEA IN MAY

The bright red sun sinks,
solemnly closing the curtain on another day

blurring the line between sky and sea,
it bathes in color its final golden scene

A young man, the breeze of May blowing over him,
stands like an iris
staring straight ahead
at that distant semicircle

Sea breeze rumpling his hair
what is he pondering so deeply?
Is he fashioning some philosophy of his own
by which to live in the future?
Is he conversing with a friend in a far-off land?
In the roar of the sea with its white waves breaking
does he seek the strength to face tomorrow?

Is he waiting to converse
with his love in the coral islands?

On the fiery sea
quietly one dot of white sail drifts

PRAYING TO MOUNT FUJI

The time for the awakening of mankind has come
the dawn!   the dawn!
the eternal light   the sacred precepts
vitality filled with rhythm
the magnificent power overflows

Mount Fuji like the dawn enriches the life of men
Mount Fuji stores within itself the everlasting spirit of holiness
its solemn form like a great sage awakening from deep
    meditation
its serene form swaying not an inch in the piercing northern
    winds
the auspicious snow that descends on it painting a picture
    of holy purity
in the fierce might of the red lord of summer never forgetting
    its gentle balm of breezes
how mighty, this graceful mountain of Fuji!

History's pages pile up a million layers deep
and the violence of war rages unabated
Where will mankind reach the shore of life,
its voyage still blocked by storms that madden the sails?

Ah, the doleful course of the globe,
hoping always for a certain guide

Those people who lived on the parched earth of the Middle
    Ages,
drawing up the clear waters of Scholasticism to restore life;
the Jews, anguished and fearful in hardship,
trusting in the coming of the Messiah, harboring their
    strength;
the people of Asia, wearied by paths of delusion,
who found the Buddha of Vulture Peak, and the flowers of
    life bloomed

Ages pass, ages come
all robes fray and grow thinner
even as the angry waves of the world grow wilder
Ah—I will pray to the sacred peak of Fuji

Those who praise Fuji—their number is unknown
I have no need for narrow-minded exaggeration
Within the century's burning hells of avarice
I stand unadorned, fearless of rebuttal
I will praise far-off Fuji
three and a half billion people, as though bowing to the
    light of the sun,
as though bathed in the mysterious radiance of the moon,
and from Mount Fuji in the distance
the sacred bells will peal and echo
The time of
freedom and peace and majesty has come
the time of awakening to life has come,
from Mount Fuji in its sacred beauty
in company with the bells of eternal peace

Oh worthy of honor—Mount Fuji,
guarding the holy writings of the True Buddha,
housing the Lord of eternal kalpas
Mighty indeed, mountain of the Saint!
for how many countless succeeding ages   key to the great
    universe
the portals of the ultimate Buddha Throne unfold
the holy bells peal and echo
the dawn!   the dawn!
the time of mankind's awakening at last has come

*Notes: Vulture Peak (p. 38) refers to Grdhrakūta, a mountain near the city
of Rajagaha in Magadha; it is also sometimes called Eagle Peak.*

*In Buddhism and Hinduism, a kalpa (p. 39) represents an immeasurably
long period of time.*

DREAMS

This morning
I had a dream of unbounded happiness
but when I woke
in an instant its phantom form vanished away

Yesterday I had a dream,
something fearful chasing me—
the memory of it lingers forever in my mind

This manifestation of "latency" that, though undirected,
assaults and takes over the entire brain—
deep in mountain fields hidden by mist,

to that person, to this friend,
this manifestation that flickers powerfully, unnaturally
on the borders of vision and reality

The life force after death,
existing as a reality
in the same sort of spatial dimension,
experiencing joy and anger, sorrow and delight,
must go through the transmigrations of birth and death

If we must dream,
we would wish for beautiful dreams

THE TRAVELER

The traveler journeys on   today again   tomorrow again
seeking the way of new fortune

What is in his heart we do not know—
does he bear a burden of sorrow?
does he bear a packet of joy?

In the cold dawn   the hot evening
the traveler presses onward, so that he may live,
lugging the weights of livelihood, buffeted by waves,
the traveler never rests, always coming from somewhere,
always bound somewhere else,
from a tragic journey, along the road of hope

Bokusui sang of it this way:
"When I've crossed countless mountains and streams, the
   land
where loneliness ends!—today again I travel on"

A society of dreams
gardens where fortune blooms
theater of the common people
dance of drama
guidelines that are certain
entrance of the chief actors

Press on, traveler!   I too make the journey,
along the endless road of mankind
from the way of anger to the way of delight

Note: *Bokusui Wakayama (1885–1928), a writer of traditional-style Japanese poetry, was admired for his elegant and romantic style.*

41

THE HEART OF THE MOON

MOONLIGHT

In the shining realm of the silver monarch
the serene light of a wonderland peace

I want to become drunk with moonlight,
not out of tender sentimentality
but as a human being living in fullest harmony with
    nature,
determined never to lose sight of its primal being,
as a natural man, unhurried,
I want to love the moonlight

From that dot at the zenith of the deep mysterious mid-
    night sky,
beams of the moon that come quietly streaming down—
in them the rigorous, unspeaking
light of the life force,
luster of those who live ever by the inherent Law—
how many stern silent counsels have I learned from it,
how many paths of encouragement?

One man sings of the full moon,
another fashions a sonata,
the Apollo spaceship reflects its face—
I want to observe the posture of the moonlight,
for that epitome of the moving universe in its stillness
I believe is the epitome of human life

Over this round garden golden waves drift lightly,
this stainless mirror gazes with the light of compassion

at the green earth as it moves and sorrows—
I love the moonlight

Not even the clouds can assault it,
not even the wind,
no shadow across the face of that flashing gold fire
Tonight again, I alone talk with the moonlight
Pondering my life with its accumulation of cares,
I watch the moonlight

THE UNIVERSE

The heavens limitless
the earth floating through the void,
not a conception, not a fancy, but actually existing,
the universe—

in times far distant
gazing at the lovely poetic radiance of the constellations,
men heard the music of fantasy

The Herd Boy sets off,
the Weaving Maiden goes to meet him, two lovers by the
    Milky Way;
at the zenith of the autumn sky, the Swan's wings spread
    in flight;
the North Star, prayer of ships on their distant voyages;
friends talking together, dancing together,
stars of the Southern Cross giving forth the sound of a lyre;

the mysterious Princess Kaguya ascending in the bright
   eighth-month moon

inscrutable space that enfolds man in its solemnity,
those far-off flickering thrones
past, present, future
in length stretching on forever,
mingling in countless dimensions,
in breadth, the music of the vast unlimited worlds
the West pursues them with the induction of science,
the East has captured them through deductive wisdom and
   meditation

The great sky with its transcendent beauty and stillness,
looking down at that distant surface
where human intellect in its anguish wanders and moves,
in the stillness of the system of fixed stars, fading yet never
   fading,
giving forth its pale blue light,
the sentient globe, alone pursuing its vast orbit

The golden waves of the sun bring to that green globe
scenes of verdure and the shifts of the four seasons,
the energy from the fusion of tiny atoms
sings of the scent of the vital and flowering life force of the
   earth

Moving, suffering, self-propelled lives
born from the cold lifeless darkness
in the lonely ages of remote antiquity,
natural vivid light and act of breathing
give proof of the living, natural pulse of the great universe

Even the magnificent swirls of the Milky Way
that counts among its kin ten solar families,
beside the endless theater of the universe
with it borderless regions measured in light years
are no more than one dot of phosphorescence
When man stands before it,
the voice of his frail and ever-fading existence dies away

As I lift up my face, dazzled,
toward those deep seas of the sky,
I stand silent and speechless,
sick with memories of anguish and abandonment

Yet the center of this vast and deep-vaulted jewel,
which even the eyes of science in their searching wisdom
could not comprehend,
the true nature of this metaphysical brilliance—
this the inner eye of the great sage of the East intuitively
    perceived
The ultimate form of the life force, eternal and primal,
which with countless millions of universes
and human existence, impermanent and ever-changing,
flows in the chaos of dim and infinitesimal atoms

Vast, boundless universe ceaselessly moving,
which can shrink to a single dot
man in his nothingness—
surrounded by its enormity,
the life force in one instant of philosophy
is about to enfold the great universe once more

The moments of cause and effect are seen simultaneously,
the limited is pregnant with limitlessness,

the instant embraces eternity,
this action, the intersection of self and universe,
each joining
in the music of the great voice of harmony,
the transformations of all beings that know no stopping

Note: The Herd Boy (p. 46), in Aquila, and the Weaver Maiden, Vega, are stars that in the Chinese mythology represent lovers parted by the Milky Way. They are permitted to meet once a year on the seventh night of the seventh lunar month.

AUTUMN WIND

By the roadside, tangled clumps of bush clover,
clear winds of autumn spring up—
among the delicate leaves,
pink and white blossoms, gentle princess faces peering

Each coming day, each coming day
was a day of trial,
panting for breath,
walking the green road, climbing upward,
on the plains, winds reveling with the pampas grass,
alone, quietly roaming the Miyagino plateau,
recalling the song of the falling star, autumn wind on
    Wu-chang Moor,
the general who died forlorn there, Chu-ko Liang

Autumn wind,
wind sighing with the wine cup of one who weeps at parting,

wind sighing with the tears in the heart of one pained,
wind with its melancholy chant to the traveler

As the crimson sun of evening dips and sinks from sight,
bell crickets sing
and the autumn wind departs

Notes: *Miyagino is a part of the Hakone National Park in Kanagawa Pre-fecture.*

Wu-chang in Shensi Province was the site where the Shu general Chu-ko Liang faced the forces of the rival state of Wei in A.D. 234, and died of illness while the battle was in progress.

PAMPAS GRASS

Beyond the bamboo grove
here and there thatch-roofed houses

Someone playing a biwa,
its notes echoing high and low

The sturdy pampas grass stands straight up,
quietly listening

A prince who laid down his life for the sovereign,
soul of a princess sorrowing with love,
come from the world of shadows
to take on pampas grass forms?

50

Moon in daytime, Naha, Okinawa ▶

Their bodies clothed in numerous delicate spikes
would the prince and princess,
just the two of them,
be lonely,
and is that why they've brought all these retainers along?

A field of pampas grasses—
Never blooming in the gaudy capital,
dressed in green trousers,
are they weary of wandering over broad meadows
and have come to rest on these hills, stretching down their
    roots?

Plumed pampas grass!
Your delicate legs like wire,
with your wrists of silver,
your golden faces,
whom are you calling to so innocently?
Do you long to hold the sleeve of one dead and gone?

Winds blow the way of flourishing and decay—
flowered pampas grass shedding teardrops of dew,
blooming in the face of the cold wind

Days of childhood
like paintings of nights under a full moon,
those dreams of moon-gazing
have grown forlorn now

How would friends of *Man'yōshū* times have sung it,
how would *Kokinshū* friends put it in a poem?

◀ *Moon and pampas grass, Hakone*

Hakone road in twilight,
the white snows of Fuji
soaring dimly

If the delicate tracery
of the painter's brush on lacquer inlay
had not caught the fields of pampas grass,
vainly
your scenes would have faded from sight

In the autumn wind, the road of glory and decline

Pampas grass,
are you gently mulling over the thoughts of old age?
Standing proud by the roadside,
on the embankment,
have you chosen to dwell out of youth's way?
While you live, do you watch as the young people pass to
a higher state?

Notes: The biwa (p. 50) is a stringed instrument resembling a lute.
The Man'yōshū, *or* Collection of Myriad Leaves *(p. 53), was the*
earliest anthology of Japanese poetry, compiled in the eighth century. The
Kokinshū, *or* Ancient and Modern Collection, *the next important*
anthology, was compiled in 805.
Hakone (p. 54) is a town situated on a lake in Kanagawa Prefecture, an
area noted for its scenic beauty.

Night

Valley stream
night wind
sound of a wind bell

Night solemnly enfolding the forest
Night, when from far beyond the bell tower
the song of human life sounds

Swallowed up in the abyss of silence,
youthful lives sleeping—
in them history's repose, when wings of combat are folded
and the primal vigor gathers itself for the flight to come

Ten thousand beings!
rest at ease,
surrendering to the night,
until the heavens shall open their golden curtain,
until the nameless plants and flowers
that cluster and bloom shall open their green eyes,
stretch out as you please,
drawing deep deep breaths

MOUNT FUJI AND THE POET

Here is a poet
a poet singing of the magnificent symmetry of Fuji

Fuji, forgive me   tonight for no reason
tears keep coming as I gaze up at you

A poet weeping
gazing up at the loftiest of the earth with its light of
    perfection

Calm days,
like a dream in the empty sky,
clouds born from it,
Fuji the object of love—
life burning deep within him,
in the flux of the Great Art,
here is a poet enamored of Fuji

Bokusui describes Fuji as the sublation of self,
solemnly sings of its eternal melody

Fuji in clear weather   shining Fuji
Fuji of white snow   soaring Fuji

Fuji sharp-outlined   Fuji in rain clouds
rough-skinned Fuji   Fuji robed in pure white

Dawn Fuji   Fuji with its cap of cloud
Fuji on a bright morning   Fuji tonight

Fuji under an oppressive sky   Fuji stretching wide
Fuji clothed in spring   Fuji naked in autumn

As a mountain of goodness, justice, and philosophy
he sings your praises in the sky

PARTING ON A CLEAR DAY

On the uplands the wind whines and sighs,
clear bright weather for our parting now,
waves of pampas grass bending white,
stirring unforgettable memories
of the summer past and the days since then

Moments of a brief lifetime,
in the shadow of the cedar rows,
by the shore of the Inland Sea,
seated at the window of a speeding train,
a friend I have known

We have opened up our thoughts to one another,
the innermost part of our thoughts—
that transparent purity that
lights up the autumn sky—
I will prize it as the finest thing in this world of ours

From this clear day, the day of parting, on,
though we may never meet again,
I will never forget—

The reality of this mutual response of heart and heart
I will continue to believe in from this moment to all time

A clear night of parting,
a cup between friend and friend,
to remember each other by, our forms reflected in it,
the moon lighting our thoughts within—
now the autumn wind comes blowing over the uplands

Time

Time—
no color to it   no scent
no form   no sound
remaining positioned
while forever and continuously passing by

Time is wordless—
a moment and yet eternal
eternal yet momentary
never lingering for an instant   without sentiment
without distance   without theory
neither the biggest nor the littlest thing
ignoring the human herd
embracing the universe it flows on

A time of anger   a time of fear
a time of delight   a time of bitterness
leaden time   vacant time
callous time   compassionate time

Yet high in the heavens above the
vibrating of the tiny life forces of the mundane world,
in the impassiveness of its transparent silence,
it strides forward with giant steps, tending its own mission

Time the controller
it is strong
it has no modesty
there is no definition greater than it

With its face like a Noh mask
it walks onward, firmly swallowing all affairs
and settling them as it goes

In this space-time are given
to the disheartened the hateful lightning
to the joyful the clear waves of golden light
to the weary the moon of resignation

That which in a brief instant
can shatter the rapt hopes of human beings,
that can reverse the swift current of society,
that can perform these miraculous and wordless deeds,
what is it in fact?
Call it the absolute controller

None among the haughty wielders of power on earth
who does not bow down before it
Even the days of proudest glory
in its presence become mere scraps of paper
To the scrambling schemes of petty humans,
a smile of derision on its face,
coldly it deals its crushing blows

Time is constancy—
Once long ago the sage of the East
through the mind of faith sought its true form,
delved into the eternity of the human world,
and at the bottom of the ever-shifting abyss of time
discovered the certain factor of constancy and permanence

Time may indeed be the controller,
but one who looks upon its vast naked countenance
will know that, as the possibility of law,
it can become man's greatest ally—so the sage taught

He who understands this principle, "time," will be strong
He who grasps the true nature of time
will be honored as the most exalted
He who comprehends the law of cause and effect,
which holds time in its breast,
can judge rightly the present and future,
for he will no longer be misled by worldly nature

Time flows
Changing, it flows unchanging
limited, it flows without limit
Hypotheses and suppositions are subsumed
under its daring metaphysical category
as, giant-visioned, it walks on
But only one who has attained the definition of this thing
    called time
can stand with time eternally
in the vanguard of history

THEME

There is a theme to each opus
and in the theme joy and sorrow echo by turns
When one has captured the clear-cut shape of the theme.
an unparalleled masterpiece may be born

There are themes to human life
and when one has discovered his own particular theme
and as an actor given it the fullest expression,
a mighty dream will be born

This thing called life—
with sweat and thoughtfulness,
as a novelist writes a novel,
with sweat and perseverance,
as a painter plies his brush,
seated before the blank paper of the instant and the future,
one creates a new portrait of oneself—
it is a vigorous task to be engaged in

SONGS OF THE REVOLUTION

Springing from the Earth

Traveler!
where have you come from?
where are you going?

The moon has set
the sun not yet risen
in the chaos before dawn
searching for the light
I press onward

To drive back the dark clouds of the mind
I seek the great tree unshaken by the storm—
will I spring up from the great earth of life?

A Believer

Nature has its clear-cut cycle of spring and fall
the globe its steady revolution of the twenty-four hours
All these
accord with the path of the eternal laws of the universe

But what are the laws of this little universe called "self"?
The stars of the heavens and the inner moral code—
so thought Kant

The ultimate law
wherein join those distant paths,

which mingles this dimension of the life within me
to the unending movements of the universe,
this I make my faith

Making my way home when scenes of turmoil are ended,
looking up at the stars that spread the sky with their
    shining,
I verify the laws that abide in the depths of my breast

And then,
while raging at the misery and injustice on this earth,
I proceed stage by stage along the path of human life, of
    birth, old age, sickness, and death
Today once more
I vow to be a true pioneer

WEEDS

They live
rank on rank of them in their green nakedness
they live vigorously
never flinching from the autumn frost, unbending in will,
through the supple resilience that is their heaven-given
    nature
they live on in joy

They live   greedily they live
never the least air of gloom about them
to the life-giving springs of the great earth their mother

calling out in answer
multiplying their friends as they live on

In the light of the heavens they live discordantly
giving thanks to the dews and springs of the earth
they live serenely

Sternly they battle with their surroundings
freely they take delight in their surroundings
day by day they carve out a life of fullness
with the drought, the gale, the drenching rain,
the morning dew, the sunset, the stars that fill the sky
they live on, dancing and singing

The burning heat relentlessly torments them,
the parching dryness, when one drop of water is a precious
    pearl,
the desperate fight—
The sudden storm in its madness would destroy them
but though they sway and bend to the ground
their chests swell with pride

The squalls attack, washing them, trying to down them,
but though their front ranks, their rear ranks are swamped,
unenraged they pick themselves up from the water

Waves of ordeal are never easy to bear
Sustained endurance in the face of life and death,
the unfaltering resistance that alone conquers all,
they who know no surrender
they who exude a thriving vitality
and they whose smiling faces never change—
even deserts are a waterside to them

even foul mud is an oasis
even barren fields are a longed-for paradise

And at last there comes to them
a time of rest

Morning dews gently call them to waking
little birds beat drums in the sky
and the light of the sun fills the grassy fields

The crimson setting sun colors them,
from the far edge of the horizon bidding them farewell,
praising them for their day's labor
and they, sitting straight up, sink into meditation

The Milky Way as it flows down the sky
speaks to them each night of dreams,
grieving over the impermanence and misfortune
of history's thousand changes, the ten thousand transforma-
    tions of life

Who is aware of the awakening
of these tiny lives?
Who salutes them from the heart?

They know nothing of hothouses
they would not wish for the tedium of the potted plant
no thoughts of flower shows occupy them
They go unadmired
unpicked—
needless to say no one would buy them
But listen
to their untroubled soliloquy,
to their intense confidence and pride!

"All artifice, all human skill,
seen in the light of the highest value, which is to live,
are mere phantoms!"
that I know is what they say to one another as they tremble
    and sway

"Such elaborate protection
such delicate love
we have no need for"

"We do not fear the gale
we do not grieve at isolation
or resent our fate"

"We leave the nightingale to his plum tree
leave the moon to lodge in the pine
to the willow we leave the spring showers"

"For the nameless
there the mission and the flowering of the nameless
for the wild, that which belongs to the wild
With our own hands
we will open up our own road
This is the beautiful road
of our green existence"

In a theater where there is no applause
endlessly, earnestly they go on giving expression
to the beauty of their gratuitous revels and parades
Ah, their name is "weeds"

How great you are
how sturdy you are
how merry you are

◀ *Late afternoon, Hamamoroiso, Kanagawa*

Green friends, who live wholehearted,
come here!
let me share my seat with you

I will watch steadily over your trials
I alone am moved to praise your vigorous truth
I want your form to be
the guideline that governs my whole life

Gazing upward at the flowing stars,
live in your own free way!
If that be the proper path,
then with the elements of your true nature just as they are
keep on forever living as you have lived

Beauty of gregariousness
strength of the indigenous
wisdom that adapts itself to circumstance

This is the unadorned world of the common people
the republican world of the human tribe
this indeed is the yearned-for world of the Serene Light

In this sky and earth from antiquity
endlessly following the rainbow,
as though sprung up from the earth,
the vigor of life!

The weeds, immersed in joy,
today again live their lives
vigorously attaining to a love that is equal, they live
in ranks, forgetting ascetic practices,
today again they live through their lives!

THE PEOPLE

Like the surging of a vast sea
stretching to the far horizon—the people

Joy, sorrow descending on them
in roaring torrents,
yet each day making some little joke,
going their way together, living on—the people

From the beginning
there's been nothing to surpass the strength and shout of the
    people
from the beginning
nothing to outrun the pace of the people's wisdom
from the beginning
nothing to rival the banners of the people's justice

Yet in the past
and today as well
the history of the people and their struggle
has been bathed in tears of suffering and want

A poet put it this way:
"While ignorance and misery remain on earth
we will never give up our fight!"

You dark wielders of power,
can you not hear the lonely sighs
of the people troubled and sickened by you?
Wise ones of the world,
can you not perceive

that a single atom
is bursting with the laws of the entire universe?
Are the masses in their long and distant wanderings
only meek, subservient objects in your sight?

"The people"—
it is a word I love

People!
why do you believe
it is your fate
solely to still the storm of the heart
and be crushed beneath the stones of tyranny?

Why do you not
cast off your ancient chains?
Have you not the right to emerge from the history of the
    dead,
to become heroes of the history of the living?

Blood that has flowed cannot be redeemed
tears that have been shed are beyond recall
Ah, but
do not be silent!
You must not resign yourselves!
You must not grow weary!
To put an end to the refrain of this stupid history
dominated by a handful of men in power,
to silence once for all this pitiful weeping,
in dancing waves of people,
for the sake of the people of the future
you must gain victory!

Now is the time
to ring down the curtain on this rainbow farce
played out by elder statesmen with their plots for
    power,
the generals rattling their sabers,
the glittering rich and mighty alone
You, looking up to the skies,
roaming the earth,
will be the leading actors on the stage now,
creating as you go a wholly different drama of history

People!
you alone are reality
Outside of you there is no real world
The age will not forget to wait and pray
for the true movement of the people

It will not forget that you alone
are the great sea into which all things flow,
the furnace, the crucible in which all things,
emerging from chaos, are refined
for the sake of a new birth,
and you are the touchstone
to distinguish truth from falsity in all things

Science, philosophy,
art, religion,
all undertakings
must be directed toward the people

Science without you is coldhearted
philosophy without you is barren

art without you is empty
religion without you is merciless

You should look down on those who sneer at you,
not be bound by those who analyze and judge others coldly,
ignore those who hate the earthy smell about you

You who work away in silence,
you with your strong muscles, browned by the sun—
I can hear the pure, rapid beating
of the heart in your breast

I will spend my life exerting myself for your sake
Though at first sight I seem to stand in isolation,
I want to make it my proud and only mission
to fight on and on for you alone,
always in your behalf

I will fight,
you will fight,
fight until the day when,
on this earth,
your rough hands will tremble
and the joy of life shines forth in your simple faces

I will fight!
You must fight too!
Wherever you may be,
holding fast to a steady tempo
today again I fight!

THE TRUTH OF MELOS

Surmounting the cliffs that rise up steeply,
tramping the vast plains of the sky,
threading through dark forests,
racing ever onward, the young man Melos

He runs, that is all—
to fulfill the firm-binding vow made with his friend,
to give proof of the quality of trustworthiness,
holding fast to the highest purity of heart, he runs on

He does not see the green trees,
he forgets the lively streets of town,
never looking up at the silver clouds,
like the dark wind he runs on

He strides forward through the midst of river waves
Clothed in robes of Truth,
praying to some great entity
whose eminence he does not understand,
he does nothing but run on and on

It is a race toward his death in the world
it is a race toward eternal rebirth

Young Melos!
You turned from the world of men,
full of falsehood and delusion,
to a rare and certain reality,
the loftiest, most beautiful, most clean

You have left behind a melody of Truth that will echo
    forever
as long as mankind shall exist

That strong Truth, wherein did it lie?
Was it in the bodily strength with which you swam the
    muddy current?
Was it in the valor with which you struck down the
    mountain robbers?

No!
for none of these penetrates to the true essence
It was in the supremacy that lies within your own heart
with which you conquered, fierce as they were,
those nightmares of fatigue that for a moment invaded your
    breast,

longings for your fond homeland,
attachments to the warmth of family,
most evil enemies within you that for a time overwhelmed
this brave man who otherwise would bow to nothing—
at that time, I know,
you must have acknowledged your frustrations
and held parley
with those deluding dreams within your heart
that secretly tempted you to pleasure and delight

But Melos rose up
for Melos had the passion of a youth
who burns for justice,
that transcends the sweet lure of vast dream fancies

He won out,
won out over himself
From past times, when the path of the convert
is threatened by bonds of affection shallow but hard to cut,
or the fear of pains too sharp to bear
and he retreats a step in despair,
then comes the logic of self-justification
that leads him to retreat still further

I have no desire
to scoff at such weakness,
to make fun of longing,
to chastise fear

It is all right if no one joins me
Observing all things objectively,
sitting upright in deep and calm thought
I would fix my eyes upon my own mission
and join the ranks of those who fight in the cause of justice

But this I would say—
in the idle ease of one who has cast off friends
there is a pain of remorse that will last to the end of life
Rather than live sorrowing in some nook or corner
forcing lonely smiles,
I would rather elect to die for Truth

One person is enough,
someone who will resist this avalanche that swallows all
    before it
For if no one resists it,

then Truth will continue forever to face defeat
and history will become a procession of fancies and falsehoods

I would remember this:
"Only the race of truly great valor
can destroy the obsessions of suspicion and scheming
and bring about the ultimate flowering of human truth"

Note: The poem is based on Run Melos!, *a short story by Osamu Dazai
(1909–48), a postwar novelist who killed himself.* Run Melos! *deals with
the Greek legend of Damon and Pythias, the latter here called Melos. The
youth Melos, having angered the tyrant Dionysius and been condemned to
death, was allowed to return home to tend to his younger sister's wedding on
condition that his best friend be held as a hostage in his place. The poem
depicts Melos's struggle to overcome various obstacles and return to the tyrant's
court by the appointed time so that his friend will not be executed in his place.
According to the legend, he succeeded in doing so and the tyrant, deeply im-
pressed with his fidelity and sense of honor, pardoned him.*

In the River of Revolution

Along with time
the fierce river of revolution flows on
today too tomorrow again too

Young man,
you who shine with a fresh new light!
It must be you and no other,
holding fast to the image in your mind

by mountains and rivers skillfully
you must build strong embankments

Young man   run!
run for the sake of the common people
run, explore the endless borders of your world

From past times sons of the revolution
with this reflection in the midst of the ultimate river,
what sort of course have they marked out?

convulsion of anger
thesis of grief
the cold laugh of irony
tear-filled eyes

And yet those youths who race in the vanguard
still in the face of this enticing challenge
display boundless fidelity

This perhaps is the destiny of youth
Young man, you do right,
for revolution in the end is a romance

Wanderings of the dreaming spirit, the kiss of romance,
upon this canvas of human life and society and history
leave vivid points and lines
the life of a painter who seems of surpassing genius—
the victory of the wisdom of the youthful revolutionary
lies in this one point

In the basic scriptures we read:
"The mind is like a skilled painter"
or again:
"I expound the teachings that move within one's own
    mind"
If expression be removed from the reality that is man
    what remains?
expression   expression   inevitable expression
expression that cannot be avoided no matter what—
reveling in this splendid freedom
Mishima cried out, Dazai died

They wanted to give expression perhaps
even to their own demise
But in the art you strive for
there is no need for such narcissism
Basic, inherent expression—
this is enough,
for this is the beauty toward which human truth gravitates

It does not matter if no one sees it
You do not need to lean on anyone
but following in accord with the single Dharma,
having faith in the true nature of your life
and the greatness of the shining victory of the Human Party
rapturously   confidently   dance your way along

We have no need of any sect
Valorously transcending the obstacles
of narrow partisanship, of cliques,
as human beings
as stark-naked human beings,
live, move, and for the sake of the joyous new society

fight, young man!
And I too will fight!

The sect of nonsectarianism
the sect called human being, which is no sect at all—
let us call this the Human Party

People perhaps may laugh
the arrogant men of power will ignore us
men of cold intellect will reject the concept

But do not grieve, friend!
They could never understand the "Human Party,"
for men drowned in the drunkenness of pride and arrogance
    and ignorance,
no image of the self
can be cast in the mirror

Do men's selves, existing only vaguely,
have so much as a fragment of compassion for the masses?
There is only barren desert there
When the light of the life force has become parched and
    dried up
it can never shine through
the shrouding mists of the world
and no clear and certain road to the future
can ever be revealed

But when you stand
upon that silent, artless, and unfathomable Dharma,
the solemn essence
that flows beneath the *Sein* of
the universe, the world, and human life,

then for the first time that clouded mirror hidden within you
will shine, be wiped clean,
and reflect the true image of you yourselves

Young man,
you are a youthful sage who has grasped this!
The ultimate world that
Goethe
Pascal
Einstein
only imperfectly glimpsed—
you are its perceiver

There is no one stronger than you
no one more trustworthy
You wear no crown perhaps
but your crownlessness should be your joy

For the overflowing power of the human being who holds
    this wisdom,
conferring no power, no wealth, no medals,
like an ultimate point of arrival—
in the depths of your heart
you embody it

Ah, human being
this unadorned reality
this upright existence
this sturdy essence that never falters or fades

Young man!
this human shout of joy,

so eloquent, so strong, so beautiful—
in the end and always you must salute it gravely,
for in it alone are the principles, the sole human likeness
of the revolutionary expression which you would fashion

And here too
in the revolutionary throb of the revolution
the revolution, in art that expands in a thousand, ten
    thousand waves,
the sublime experiment exists here, I believe
And here alone will the light that comes with the
manifestation of the revolution of wisdom appear

Flowing from its springs
the joyful life of revolution
making flowers of awakening bloom out of anguish,
the springtime of revolution—
these in their pure, strong gladness
are the days of the revolution

In the youthful heart, so long sought for,
the tidal waves of excitement and elation—
when they surge forth from this shore to that
then the eternally flowing river of the revolution
will change into a magnificent torrent

This will be the society no one has ever seen before
the homeland that everyone has sought

Then men for the first time
will emerge from the shiftings of the dark night
to return to themselves

and mankind too
will reach the oasis, reversion to the primal

And you who,
in the midst of the river of revolution that moves toward
    the twenty-first century,
grip the rudders of sagacity and justice,
it will be your skill that brings this about

Notes: Yukio Mishima (p. 82), 1925–70, was a novelist and playwright who committed ritual suicide after failing in an attempt to enlist support for his right-wing ideology.
    Sein (p. 83) is German for "existence."

SONG OF BUILDING

Ah, the sun rises resplendent
in time to the beat of a new life
Arising, builders, fighters,
we will sing a song of building!
Seven-colored clouds are streaming
ah, the morning bell peals out

The forest of giant cedars
takes on the hue of gold
tree rings from seven hundred years past
cut through so many layers
This year   this dawn
this moment so long waited for

Sun over the ocean, Hamamoroiso, Kanagawa ▶

when one has unveiled his own treasure tower
then another must erect
his treasure tower as well

With compassion, endurance, daring
fighting souls endowed with a glorious determination
never to be matched in past or future
for never has the call to action rung out so clear

The forest of giant cedars
seven hundred lonely years has waited for this moment
now in time to the builders' hammer beats
its treetops tremble with a delight
like the joy we humans find in life

For treasure towers unknown in man's ten thousand
    years
that shining primal fire
to be lit in this instant
We stand in files
treasure towers of high repute, like sands of the Ganges
in each of our lives
let the torches flare forth!

We advance to the mark, builders, friends
we live for our mission, brave builders
the prophetic torches like signal fires
lift them high to the sky, carry them ever onward!

Notes: *This poem was published in the New Year's Day issue of the* Seikyō
Shimbun *in January, 1969, three months after work was begun on the con-
struction of the Shō-Hondō, or Grand Main Temple, of Taisekiji. President*

Ikeda led the movement to build the Shō-Hondō as an expression of the desire for world peace and the happiness of mankind.

In Indian mythology, the ashura (p. 90) were originally benevolent deities who later came to be regarded as evil. In Buddhism, the ashura represent one of the six lower states of existence, that characterized by anger. They are depicted as ugly, giant in size, and dressed in armor, carrying on continual warfare with Indra and the other gods.

SOUNDS OF INNOVATION

The waves shine
the dawn has come
the dawn of innovation
to the sound of the masses singing

Now we pass through
the main gate of glory
straining ears to the beat of building hammers—
carrying out an innovation never known before—
its name is *kōsen-rufu*

If the one man's call of holy wisdom be true,
as one wave gives rise to ten thousand,
so in the breast of each of
mankind's three and a half billions
that call will echo and resound

One call of holy wisdom's truth,
though it may seem to fade into the vastness of the sky,
as ripples spread on the surface of the water,

will not fade away but become an echo,
an echo calling forth more echoes
until at last they join to form a splendid symphony

Ah, that sound from seven hundred years past,
that is our popular movement
About us the dark skies of the century's end,
here alone the torch of life shines brightly

In the night sky of our world, with its wintry blasts,
the only beacons that give forth light
are those kindled by our nightly meetings
Where the pulse of innovation beats,
there the fires flare up brighter and brighter
Let our meetings
unfold their flowers in splendor!

Buds that swell
amid the sound of lively talk and laughter,
bright open faces of this person, that person, another person,
brilliant understanding   outpouring passion
at such times treasure towers of life rise majestically

Murmur of the pulse of innovation
in the night sky of the century's end
softly calls to the dawn
"When darkness is deepest
daybreak is near"

This instant when we wait the dawn,
from northern borders buffeted in snow,
to the end of the south where rape flowers bloom,

our meetings that band together and dance with joy,
with the pulse of life bright for seven hundred years,
let their myriad blossoms flower in pride!

Ah, countless flowers bloom in the gardens of the common
    people
While the pulse of innovation sounds its beat
it prepares to open up forcefully the posture of human life
Lively dialogue—
amid the dialogue of life force and life force
the powers of the past fume and splutter
and established values are overturned
This is where the rebirth of the masses begins

Innovation is rebirth
rebirth is reversion of the life force
The call of the holy wisdom of one man
does not fade in the sky but is now substantiated

Men struggle desperately
to become men once more
but their struggle fades away in vain like foam
Only the cry of that one man
only the cry of that holy wisdom
becomes the sound of rebirth—why should this be?

Men's strivings, which are the pursuit of the life force—
when they reached their fartheast point,
there was the cry of holy wisdom
As a single sound sets in motion waves of sound,
so where this cry has echoed for seven hundred years
there have been countless millions of rebirths

Ah, decade of the 1970's!
from the end of this century
toward the twenty-first century time flows swiftly
   onward
and the pulse of innovation too shall flow
The overture has begun,
the symphony of the life force never heard before—
Beat and thunder the drum of passion!
blow the flutes of wisdom!
play upon the strings of intellect!
let their splendid sounds
roll and reach to the ends of heaven and earth!
Ah, my friends,
my friends in innovation!

Let us mount white horses   gallop in haste
where those sounds roll forth
set up numberless flashing beacons
that will send out boundless beams of light
adorning these ranging islands of Japan
bringing innovation to the destiny of each one of
mankind's three and a half billions
Let us guard the peace and prosperity of all men in their
   rebirth

UNCROWNED FRIENDS

You, my uncrowned friends, full of pride,
in the morning stillness
gazing up at the dawn sky, with the message of the faith,

carrying it forward again today   again tomorrow
You are the envoys of the Buddha
true monarchs of the multitude

Not those basking in fame but the unseen toilers,
you are the ones I will never forget!
for I too once ran that same course
In that bitter battle at Waterloo
England won,
the French forces at last defeated,

but Victor Hugo demanded to know,
who was the true winner?
He who faced the cannon of the allies
defiant, never surrendering,
one man fighting bravely and falling,
the unknown soldier, Cambronne

Who was it raised the true song of triumph?
Not the generals, not the officers,
but that valiant uncrowned fighter for life,
that stubborn soldier of the rank and file

History is not formed and moved forward
by the lone hero
but by those who fight with their lives, the unseen men
and the advancement of the faith's propagation too follows
    this principle
You are the ones I rely on!
You are our pillars, engines that propel its movement

It is you I sing in praise of

Others in time will surely honor you
as foremost among the builders and accomplishers
who spread the message of the Wonderful Law

Culture and the Great Earth

A new century
century of life—in time to its symphony
the primal sun rises
piercing the dark of ignorance,
in splendor it ascends

Now   drenched in the sunlight of limitless compassion
the great earth forty years sown with the Wonderful Law,
while we talk together
this new world made by our hands—
in the dawn we see, here in its fertile plain
new shoots of joy, sweet-smelling.
piercing the earth's crust, leaping up

New shoots from the earth,
the endurance of their long winter sleep is ended
Spring with its burgeoning grasses has come
Young shoots dotting the great earth, each on its
own throne at last, deep-rooted,
no more to know what it means to wither

Flowers unfolding, vivid with green,
you young plants of life
lushly, strongly lift your fresh leaves to the sky!

You seedlings who one after another
still spring forth smartly,
forsake isolation for the bonds of union,
here and now let us transform the earth
into a carpet of new shoots!

Stand but once on the emerald earth,
ah, gaze far off
to the very edge of that distant horizon—
the stage of those green new shoots lies completed
Now upon it an eternal melody,
a song of health, of fortune, of pride,
scored by the common people,
beneath the baton of the common people,
with the common people let us sing in chorus, let us dance
    on!

Grow, you shoots sprung from the earth!
Cherry, plum, peach, damson,
grow with all your might, each in his own way!

Victor Hugo cries:
"This century will be great and strong,
a noble impulse will guide it!"
This advent, world harmony,
the multitudes have been waiting for its day

Despondency at man's infinite smallness,
manifestations of paralysis inbred in the masses,
destruction of the people's culture

A society sick with fraud and illusion
a globe rent and torn by hate

Faced with the whirling waters of this abyss,
conquering ennui and alienation,
let us cross over, transcend them by the bridge of the
    Wonderful Law

For the sake of life and culture,
through thought and action we will create
and put into practice measures for relief

Not a bridge of rainbows, a thing of dreams,
but finer than rainbows, lovelier,
a bridge adamantine and indestructible we will build

A bridge of culture longed for from antiquity,
for history's laws have decreed the death of the old culture
We stand at the gate from which an epochal popular culture
    will emerge

Upon this desert of the spirit
to pour the waters of awakening—
this task shall be the forefront of our faith
This indeed is the great undertaking of the century,
till the end of time to spread the teachings abroad

In the very midst of the century's quakes and shocks
we must pull up, cast away the wretched roots of barbarism
The struggle between barbarism and humanity—
this is what I would call culture

Now   the century is swamped in false culture
and in the roots of vanity
the devil wallows

Senseless warfare and slaughter
nuclear warheads aimed who knows where?
a world beginning to rot with pollution—
ah, these floods of barbarism!

Young shoots!
young shoots sprung from the earth!
Who has called forth your worthy selves?
Who on this great earth
has sent the winds of bliss and purity blowing
and with the blazing rays of the eternity-old sun set you
    growing?

If you would know for certain,
now is the time
to recall the everlasting vow

Through the fulfillment of our mission
the destiny of mankind shall be transformed
A future of honor and glory dwells therein
If, weighed down by the pressures of past centuries,
we cower hidden in trenches of seclusion
we call forth a century of atrocious barbarism

Challenge the discord of hope and despair
all forms of barbarism
take away the poison from the air
take away the poison from the water
take away the poison from the grain
pluck the evil talons from the atom
dispel the dark of ignorance from mankind!

This in truth is the wish we hold in common
the imperative of the time
Upon its advancement society rests its hopes
and from its heart gives assent
For the sake of this we spread the teachings abroad

Ah, our historic generation—
it must not fall prey to the avarice
of a handful of men in high power!
Mankind's heritage with all its values
must not be left to the hands of barbarous violence!

Deathless young shoots sprung from the ground,
lift the banner of unflinching faith,
grow quickly to be great trees!
Be great trees living as individuals,
draw up sustenance from the earth of the Wonderful Law,
let it spread to the very tips of your branches

A vista of a thousand miles—
by the banks of the rivers of art and literature
on the mountaintops of science and philosophy
in the barren plain of politics
the steamy swamp of economics
in the family garden of a single home
you must grow to be great lofty trees!

Young shoots, my friends,
contend with and endure the storms of barbarism
build the true culture!
If cultivation
be the primal aim of culture,

do not forget the blessings of the great earth of philosophy
Not permitting a single person to be sacrificed
you must go forward in triumph
If the struggle with every form of barbarism
be the function of culture,
you dare not forget the mission of those sprung from the earth
Look!
in the vista before us,
young shoots sprung from the earth,
growing to a forest of giant trees
And when myriad-clustered blossoms adorn their limbs,
along the thousand-mile paths of green
in the direction of the teaching of the True Buddha,
treasure towers of the culture of the life spring into view!

We move, putting on the crowning doctrine
today again   tomorrow again
toward the unfolding of the new century of life

Extending the movement of the Great Religion—
this is the tide of the great cultural movement,
and in its surging current
shall be joined the tributaries of education, politics,
    economics

This moment
when the destiny of the globe at last is changing
shall become the holiday of rebirth, peace, and prosperity
This shall be
the true, the highest culture—the fulfillment of our faith

To Those Who Guard the Dignity of Life

Freedom, peace, dignity—
women have been the fighters for these emblems

from times of high antiquity
holding life to be of priceless value
with unrivaled tenderness
taking pains, nourishing
faithful for a lifetime to these high principles—
these I call true women!

These same pure partisans of peace
have been sucked under in the muddy torrents of a violent
    society
driven at times to idiocy, at times to frenzy
at the mercy of the muddy waves
bobbing, sinking
suffering, gasping
through the long, long years

But you have taken leave of that ancient scene
dance now in a new earth and sky
bathed in joy and wisdom and fortune
now before the cloudless mirror of the Lotus
you view yourselves

That pure life you see there
beautifully, warmly, richly
shall love and nourish all beings—
the people trust in your determination

Family, society, truth—
following that golden road without regret
taking pains, nourishing noble figures
gentle and well-loved
at times as wives
at times as mothers
you are the true queens of the harmonious families

Now in the dawn of this century of life
how many millions of women shining in glory
how many billions of harmonious families
by those hills and rivers
these hills and rivers too blooming like flowers
Then the earth made ugly and cruel
I know will stand before that mirror,
the purity of the Wonderful Law,
and correct its posture

With unity, happiness, liberation
most steadily, most swiftly
you yourselves guard the dignity of life
Eternal peace and prosperity—
these are not something far far away
they are there in the pure power within your breasts!

WORDS OF ENCOURAGEMENT

The sun rises   the moon shines serenely
Young man!   Never give in to your despondent self
but open wide the castle gates of your being
and hold commerce with another world

*

The moon watches beautifully
Even amid their cares,
friends who talk earnestly together
in them the flowers of the life force
will bloom and send forth fragrance forever

*

Trusted without limit by others,
who say of me,
"He seems to have fun
and there's an uprightness to him,"
standing tall,
a broad-minded man—
that I would be to the end of my life

*

Like the sun
always bright in heart,
like the sea
with a heart vast and wide,
like the sky
with a heart unendingly tall,
like the flowers
with a heart forever beautiful,

with a heart set on happiness,
like the wind
be free!

⁂

By day an ordinary man in society,
each day I work to make a living.
By night, companion of the moonlight,
philosopher of the common people,
singing of life,
steadily I advance down the silver road

⁂

Bathed in the evening sun,
you set off on foot for the discussion meeting—
that in future you may .chart a worthy course
with a solemnity like that of your figure,
I would sketch you

⁂

Facing the distant sun,
now on the point of setting,
off to talk with the people of their worries—
your golden life and activity
I would stretch out my arms to

⁂

Though they may be days of
fierce fighting for the revolution,
when the seasons come round I can never forget
the kerria rose, the bush clover, the iris—
I want to be a youthful poet

Anyone can intone the chant
of the dignity of life—
the important thing,
with this destined existence,
the grave fact of life on earth,
one corner of the great universe,
is to ask how much joy and humility is in that life—
the answer will determine if it is creative or a mere sham

                    ❊

No greater fool than one
who submits weeping to destiny
Only the style of life that
flings a clear challenge to destiny
is capable of transforming it

                    ❊

As the ceaseless waves keep pounding
till they've broken down the rocks,
so I would go on striving to destroy established evils,
working all my life long,
never letting up

                    ❊

Young man!
let us spend today again
talking with the poor, the common people,
for only among these masses of humanity
are true poetry, true painting,
true music to be found

One does not choose the peaceful flower garden paths,
but advances by one's own will on the road of thorns,
hoping thereby to create
life unending, hot with tears

⁓

"Come into this lovely garden!"
I say, calling gently to those suspicious-hearted people—
that is the kind of full, rich life
I have lived once again today

⁓

So that you may continue to possess
those beautiful eyes,
that beautiful hair,
that beautiful heart,
today again
live tautly, taut in faith

⁓

Though today's hopes
may not be easy to fulfill,
in the world of tomorrow the new moon shines
and Mount Fuji to me
glows with the color of gold

⁓

No glittering exalted eminence
has ever been my dream
As a friend of the little people
to build a society of equality
that beams with the light of human victory—
this is my creed

Admiring the cherry blossoms,
admiring the chrysanthemums,
bringing to bloom the flowers
of happiness within the heart,
even on days of rain and cloud,
confidently we will go forward!

※

Like the waterfall   fierce
like the waterfall   unflagging
like the waterfall   unfearing
like the waterfall   merrily
like the waterfall   proudly—
a man should have the bearing of a king

※

I have determined
to climb that mountain
Therefore, choosing firm footholds day by day
I go forward
Because I know that to look lightly on reality
may mean disaster,
I work hard at my faith

※

I will be a beacon light,
a small and yet a great light
that the people can trust and take ease in

The "weathermark" identifies this book as a production of John Weatherhill, Inc., publishers of fine books on Asia and the Pacific. Supervising editor: Miriam F. Yamaguchi. Book design and typography: Meredith Weatherby. Production supervisor: Mitsuo Okado. Printing of the text: Kinmei, Tokyo. Engraving and printing of the plates, in four-color offset: Nissha, Kyoto. Binding: Makoto, Tokyo. The typeface used is Monotype Perpetua, with hand-set Perpetua for display.

DATE DUE

AUG 4 2001

DEMCO 38-297

The beat of builders' hammers echoes sharply
We pass through the gate of glorious dawn
gazing up at white snows of Fuji
hastening now to complete an unprecedented propagation
fifty transmissions performed from person to person
files of treasure towers, some fifteen million lives
making ourselves the base of this propagation
leaping in joy, treading the great earth

The base—make it deep, make it deeper
that the sacred fire for countless kalpas to come
may shine in splendor
a base, a foundation that will never crumble
We will build it now!

Look back at the stream of the past—
Babylon's waters long gone dry
the moon setting over Greece
lighting the ruins of Egypt and Rome
the sacred Ganges once more muddied
the long walls of China turned to useless ribbons
every temple and hall of the past
crumbling away, transformed by the turning years

Destruction—a matter of a moment
building—a struggle to the death
inertia is darkness, hope is light
retreat is death, advance is life

Ah, twenty years and more
since the True Law almost passed away

◀ *Sunset, Tokyo*

Among the mountains and rivers of a ruined land
this lone great master of mine faced the broad plain, gave
    his shout—
Return to the past of the True Buddha
now amid the beat of builders' hammers
I too shall shout with all the voice I have—
Return to that great master who stood on the broad plain!
So will we return to the past of the True Buddha

In destruction, the iron helmets of ashura
in building, the iron helmets of the establishers of right
above our heads it burns in brightness
the blinding body of the Wonderful Law

The base—make it deep, make it deep
dig to the very roots of the rock
Beneath the temples of antiquity
how many millions of human beings lay buried in sacrifice?
Now at the base of this edifice we build
pack in all the glory of human life
different bodies made one in heart
forests of treasure towers, vessels of our lives
let them adorn this temple where peace beats its wings

This forest of the treasure towers of our lives
when it burgeons and shines in our trailing islands of the east
here in one corner of the universe—
in dreams we've seen it—
we shall build the new society of the Pure Paradise!

But now when the world hovers upon heartless destruction
our building permits no dreams
firmly we build for the peace of myriads